God's Word in My Breath

A devotion for what YOU need exactly when YOU need it

By La'Tosha M. Aikens

God's Word in My Breath
A devotion for what YOU need exactly when YOU need it.

Softcover edition ISBN: 979-8-2841100-4-1
Aikens, La'Tosha M.
God's Word in My Breath
A devotion for what YOU need exactly when YOU
need it. Email: slaikens15@gmail.com
The versions of the Bible used are as follows:
NLT-New Living Translation
ESV-English Standard Version
NKJV-New King James Version
NIV-New International Version
KJV-King James Version
MSG-Message

Cover design logo by Steven Aikens
Author photo courtesy of JR Logan

Dedication

To my beloved husband,

Steven,

You are a constant reminder of God's grace and love in my life. Your unwavering faith, patience, and support have been my anchor through every season. This book is as much a reflection of your strength and devotion as it is of mine. I thank God daily for the gift of you—my partner, my provider, my protector, my best friend, my greatest encourager.

May we continue to walk together in faith, growing deeper in love and in the knowledge of His truth.

With all my heart,

La'Tosha

Table of Contents

Introduction: The Complexity of Emotions

Often, we see a smile and assume it signals happiness, or we see tears and immediately think of sadness. These emotions seem so clear-cut, don't they? But what if I told you that you could smile and weep at the same time? That you could feel grateful and sad simultaneously? Or perhaps experience jealousy and shame in a single moment? This, my friend, is what I call *complex emotions*.

We often fail to recognize the depth of our emotional lives. We can feel more than one emotion at once, whether directed at a person or a situation. Sometimes those emotions are contradictory—joy and sorrow, hope and frustration—and yet they coexist within us, shaping our experience. The beauty of this complexity is that, even in our emotional turmoil, God has given us grace to bear more than one emotion at a time.

The challenge, however, is learning how to process these emotions. What matters most is how we allow ourselves to sit with them and work through them. I remember a season in my own life where I experienced this profound emotional complexity. I was filled with joy as new opportunities opened before me, yet there was a deep sadness as I watched old chapters close. I was grateful that God was guiding me through it all, even though the process was difficult. It was a time when my emotions seemed to be pulling me in different directions, but I chose to be still, to breathe, and to let God show me how to navigate it all.

This book is born from that experience. It's a journey through the many emotions we encounter on a day-to-day basis, and it's an invitation for you to take a moment to pause and reflect on the emotions you may be carrying. The purpose of this devotional is not to simplify the emotional journey, but to give you space and time to recognize that God's Word, combined with your breath, has the power to transform your perspective on whatever emotions you're dealing with right now.

As you journey through these pages, my hope is that you will gain a deeper understanding of your own emotional complexity, and allow God's grace to guide you in processing your feelings. Whether you're navigating joy, sorrow, frustration, or peace—know that God is with you, and He is big enough to carry it all.

Let's begin this journey together.

Why Using Different Names of God Is Important:

Each name of God helps to reveal a different facet of His character and nature. As we pray or meditate on these names, we can:

1. **Deepen Our Understanding of God**: Knowing God's different names help us understand the fullness of His character and His relationship with His people.

2. **Strengthen Our Faith**: When we face particular struggles—be it in healing, provision, peace, or protection—we can call on the specific name of God that aligns with our need, helping us trust in His ability to meet that need.

3. **Enhance Our Worship**: Praising God by using His names helps us connect with Him in more personal and intimate ways, acknowledging His greatness and His nearness.

4. **Increase Spiritual Awareness**: Meditating on the various names of God can help with developing a broader and richer understanding of God's presence in all aspects of our lives.

By using these names intentionally in prayer, we better understand the vastness of God's character and the different ways He works in our lives.

Different Names of God

Abba-Father

Adonai-Lord or Master

Yahweh-God

Jehovah- God

Elohim-Mighty One

Jehovah Nissi-The Lord is My Banner

El Roi-The God who see me

Jehovah Tsidkenu-The Lord is our Righteousness

Jehovah Machsi-The Lord my Refuge

El Elyon-Most High

El Olam-Forever or Everlasting

Alpha and Omega-Comprehensiveness of God

El Chay-The Living God

El Deah-The God of Knowledge

Immanuel-God with us

Messiah-The Anointed One

El Chuwl-The God who gave you birth

Jehovah Shammah-The Lord is there

Jehovah Tsuri-The Lord is my Rock

Bible Devotional Guide Day 1:

Topic: Trust

Read: Proverbs 3:5-8 NLT

Key Verse: "Trust in the Lord with all your heart; do not depend on your own understanding. Seek His will in all you do, and He will show you which path to take."

Apply:

In our journey of faith, there is an ever-present invitation from God to trust in His unfailing love and faithfulness. Trust is not always easy, especially when we face uncertainties, challenges, or disappointments.

Trusting in the Lord requires surrendering our desires, ambitions, and fears. It means acknowledging that His ways are higher and wiser than our own. Just as a child trusts their loving parent, we are called to place our trust in the One who created us, knows us intimately, and has a perfect plan for our lives.

When we trust in God, we acknowledge His sovereignty and His unwavering faithfulness. It is an act of surrender, releasing our need for control and embracing His guidance. Trusting in God doesn't mean that we will never face difficulties or trials, but it does mean that we can be rest assured that He is with us in every circumstance. We can find peace and strength knowing that He is working together all things for our good who are called by His name. -Romans 8:28

Moreover, having trust in God is not passive; it requires active participation. We are called to seek His guidance, study His Word, and listen to His voice through prayer. As we cultivate a deeper relationship with Him, our trust grows stronger, and we become more attuned to His will.

Trusting in God involves aligning our desires with His, patiently waiting for His perfect timing, and taking steps of faith, even when the path is unclear.

Ultimately, let us make a decision to trust in God with our whole hearts. Let us rest in the knowledge that He is faithful and always has our best interests at heart.

Pray:

Dear Heavenly Father, I come before You today, acknowledging Your faithfulness and sovereignty over my life. Help me to surrender my desires, fears, and plans to You, trusting that You have a perfect plan for me. In moments of uncertainty, grant me the peace that surpasses all understanding. Amen.

Further reading: Psalm 37:3-7, Psalm 56:3-4, Isaiah 26:3-4, Jeremiah 17:7-8

Ponder:

☐ Are there benefits of trusting God's plan for us?

☐ How easy is it to trust in God entirely?

☐ What are you currently trusting God for?

My reflection.

The thoughts that stood out to me are: DATE _____

_____

_____

_____

_____

_____

_____

_____

_____

_____

_____

_____

_____

_____

_____

_____

_____

La'Tosha M. Aikens

Bible Devotional Guide Day 2:

Topic: Joy

Read: Philippians 4:4 ESV

Key Verse:

"Rejoice in the Lord always; again, I will say, rejoice."

Apply:

Joyfulness is a state of the heart. Joy cannot be fully expressed by words alone. It comes from within the heart and bursts out of your being. A joyful heart is a heart that completely believes in God's promises and is grateful for ALL things. Joy is a fruit of the Spirit (Galatians 5:22) and can never be expressed in fullness until we have come to understand what it really is.

Joy is not just a mere feeling of happiness. What the world considers as joy can be compared with the term "trade by barter," and it refers to the exchange of one thing for another. In other words, we become joyful when we receive gifts, get good grades, a good job, a new house, etc., but when life becomes tough, when we don't get what we hoped for, when we lose our job, etc. we become sad and lose our joy.

While all this is true of what can give us joy, they are yet temporal, and thus will get to a point when they no longer bring us joy. As children of God, we are meant to understand that the joy that the Holy Spirit gives is the joy of the Lord. It never fades by circumstances; it is fresh, pure, and sweet daily. This is due to the knowledge of the Source of that joy. Understand, therefore, that this joy is such that humankind cannot give, it can only be fully expressed in a life that knows the Lord. This joy gives strength, peace, fellowship with the Father, etc. This joy has the understanding that amidst life's trials and circumstances, we can never fall, for the Lord holds us dearly in His embrace. We are rest assured of God's love and this gives us joy like a river.

If your soul is satisfied in Christ, you will rejoice in Christ. Take your eyes off Christ, and you'll lose your joy. If you lose such joy, it could just be a sign that you've turned to look at the situation more than you're looking at the One who can fix it.

Paul and Silas were in jail, and instead of thinking of their imprisonment and feeling bad about it, they knew their Source of strength and joy. So they sang and prayed, and the Bible says the prison gate opened with an earthquake. Can you really picture this scene? I always felt Paul and Silas danced while singing and praying, and were heedless that they were locked up. This day, practice being joyful always and find your joy in God.

Pray:

Lord, thank You so much for teaching me about Your joy and that all I ever need is in You. As I walk today, fill me with Your joy and fill my family, too, with Your joy. Let me work better today in the understanding of Your love for me, amen.

Further reading: Nehemiah 8:10, Romans 15:13, Psalm 16:11, James 1:2-3, Proverbs 10:28, Psalm 47:1.

Ponder:

☐ What does joy mean to you?

☐ What does it mean to experience joy in the midst of trials?

☐ Has there ever been a time when you could not find joy within?

My reflection.

The thoughts that stood out to me are: DATE _____

La'Tosha M. Aikens

Bible Devotional Guide Day 3:

Topic: **Silence**

Read: **Matthew 26:62 NKJV**

Key Verse:

"And the high priest arose and said to Him, "Do You answer nothing? What is it these men testify against You?" But Jesus kept silent. And the high priest answered and said to Him, "I put You under oath by the living God: Tell us if You are the Christ, the Son of God!"

Apply:

The Bible teaches us that there is a time under the earth when we ought to speak or remain silent (Ecclesiastes 3:7). In today's world, remaining silent, especially in the face of opposition, is considered weakness or lack of courage and so, it becomes necessary to defend oneself in the face of any slightest provocation. While some respond to provocations, others find it difficult to bridle their tongue even for a few minutes.

Our words can make or break us, and that is why Proverbs 15:4 teaches us to bridle our tongue for it can make or break us or our neighbors. The Bible calls a person who is unable to control their tongue unwise for they make themselves vulnerable to the devil's schemes. A typical example we see in the scriptures is the life of Samson who, with the words of His mouth, led to His downfall.

We must also be mindful of the stillness of the mind. As children of God, the devil stages war in our minds to prevent us from knowing God's will. Each time, with any given matter, he intentionally creates noise with distractions that makes us less discerning. We must learn to walk by The Spirit so that we may not gratify the desires of the flesh.

Today's scripture shows us how Jesus kept silent amidst all the words spoken to Him. He was provoked; He was inflicted; He was accused. Yet, in the face of all this, He knew the will of His Father was for Him to suffer that persecution for our sake, and so He remained silent to the questions asked by the priests and the scribes. This not only infuriated them, but also it made them marvel at what kind of a man Jesus was.

Keeping silent, therefore, doesn't depict weakness but strength and shows self-control. On the other hand, keeping silent out of fear or not wanting to say the truth in love, or not giving justice by speaking rightly over a matter can be considered bad. Carefully reflect on these things and rather than speaking without control, listen more today (James 1:19).

Pray:

Abba Father, teach me to remain silent when necessary and when to speak up. Help me by Your Word to remain steadfast in seeking your face. Give me wisdom at every point in time so that I don't become prey to the devil's ploys. In Jesus' name, amen.

Further reading: Psalm 141:3, Proverbs 10:19, Ecclesiastes 5:2, Proverbs 17:28, Colossians 4:6.

Ponder:

- ☐ Does silence imply weakness? Why or why not?

- ☐ Is it right to remain silent at all times?

- ☐ Has there ever been a time when you should have been silent and weren't?

My reflection.

The thoughts that stood out to me are: DATE _____

_____

_____

_____

_____

_____

_____

_____

_____

_____

_____

_____

_____

_____

_____

_____

_____

_____

_____

Bible Devotional Guide Day 4:

Topic: **Submission**

Read: **James 4:7 NIV**

Key Verse:

"Submit yourselves, then, to God. Resist the devil, and he will flee from you."

Apply:

To submit means bringing oneself under a higher authority over him or her. Submission by God's designation was for humankind to become accountable and subjected to a higher authority over us for accountability. By God's divine plan, He created us to worship Him and submit to His rulership over our lives. God has also given us the power of free will but expects our total worship and submission to Him.

According to God's Word, today we learn four places the Bible teaches us to submit and follow authority. Submission to God's authority (Romans 13:1), spouse's submission to one another (1 Peter 3:1-7), submission to authorities above us (1 Peter 2:13) and servant's submission to their masters (1 Peter 2:18). When we submit, it shows the state of humility of our heart. God rightly orders our steps and teaches us the way to go (Isaiah 30). Submission is a key to unlocking the favor and plans towards us. It brings peace, joy, and a place of rest in God.

Submission becomes difficult when we fail to regard God's Lordship over our lives. We become a tool of rebelliousness just like Satan, and God hates the spirit of rebellion. Absalom, King David's son, rebelled against his father, and this led to his own death. Rebelliousness opens the door to sins like pride, self-justification, anger, etc. We live in a sinful world in which our flesh wants to gratify the desires of this world where rebelliousness is part. Scripture says the person who is a friend with the world is in enmity with God. James 4:4 It becomes difficult to submit to God's plan and purpose, especially when it doesn't align with the world view. But we must overcome this, for anyone who is led by the flesh becomes a slave to sin and death. But if you walk in obedience and submission with the help of the Spirit, it leads to a more fulfilled life here on earth and still gives us life in the life after. We must, therefore, desire to please the Lord by submitting to our spouses, or any authority set over us.

Jesus submitted His will to His Father and by this, all humankind was saved. Submission is not always pleasurable, especially in the face of decision-making. But when we obey, God is pleased with us, and we reap the blessings set for those who obey.

Pray:

Almighty, we pray today to You who teaches us by Your word to be submissive. Help us, Lord, to become submissive to You, our spouses, and other authorities above us. This is the right way, so that in the end, we will glorify Your name. Amen.

Further reading: Ephesians 5:21, 1 Peter 5:5, Romans 13:1, Colossians 3:18, Hebrews 13:17.

Ponder:

- ☐ What happens when you submit as a child of God?

- ☐ How do you know when you are not submitting to God's will for your life?

☐ Why then do I find it constantly difficult to submit to His will? Does my will align with His will?

My reflection.

The thoughts that stood out to me are: DATE _____

_____

_____

_____

_____

_____

_____

_____

_____

_____

_____

_____

_____

_____

_____

_____

_____

_____

Bible Devotional Guide Day 5:

Topic: **Enemies**

Read: **Matthew 5:43-48 NIV**

Key Verse:

"You have heard that it was said, 'Love your neighbor and hate your enemy.' But I tell you, love your enemies and pray for those who persecute you, that you may be children of your Father in heaven. He causes his sun to rise on the evil and the good, and sends rain on the righteous and the unrighteous."

Apply:

An enemy is someone who despises you, and perhaps, you despise them, too. It most often feels justified to hate a person who hates you. However, Jesus instructs us to love those who persecute us or try to hurt us, hoping that God will touch their hearts and change them.

John 10:10 says the thief comes to kill, steal, and destroy. This is solely the devil's job description; we must therefore realize that he is the real enemy and that he uses the tools that are available to him. It could be your boss at the office, your teacher in school, your colleagues, etc. Most often, these are unbelievers, while other times, they could be God's children who do not guard their hearts.

In Ephesians 6:10–20, we learn that the weapons of our warfare are not carnal 2 Corinthians 10:4; in other words, we must understand that to win a war with the real enemy, we must understand his tactics. When we start hating our boss or colleagues and think of ways of harming them because they've harmed us, we fight the wrong battle and become prey to the devil.

Ephesians teaches us that such an individual is under the devil's attack, and as such, we must pray for a change of heart and rescue of that person's soul from the devil's claws. When we do this, we defeat the devil's plan to keep the wrong adversary and fight the genuine enemy. This is not always easy, but with the help of the Holy Spirit, just like Jesus, we can love those that hate us and whom the devil has enslaved in enmity towards us, and pray that they be delivered. Today, live in love and ask the Holy Spirit to help you.

Pray:

Adonai, You've opened my eyes today to see the real enemy. Help me fight against every war he brings. Teach me to love, understand, and help those who I previously thought were my enemies, and help me put on the full armor of God to fight against the devil and his agents, Amen.

Further reading: Proverbs 25:21, Romans 12:20, Luke 6:27-28.

Ponder:

- ☐ Who then is my real enemy and what is he after?

- ☐ What should I do when my neighbors or my friends are in enmity with me?

- ☐ How do you know when someone is an enemy?

My reflection.

The thoughts that stood out to me are: DATE _____

_____

_____

_____

_____

_____

_____

_____

_____

_____

_____

_____

_____

_____

_____

_____

Bible Devotion Guide Day 6

Topic: Envy

Read: James 3:13-16 NIV

Key Verse:

"Who is wise and understanding among you? Let them show it by their good life, by deeds done in the humility that comes from wisdom. But if you harbor bitter envy and selfish ambition in your hearts, do not boast about it or deny the truth. Such "wisdom" does not come down from heaven but is earthly, unspiritual, demonic. For where you have envy and selfish ambition, there you find disorder and every evil practice."

Apply:

One of the very traits that God is displeased with is envy. Desiring what someone else has may not be with a wrong motive. But when that bitter feeling begins to set in, or the belief that we ought to be the one in that position or in possession of whatever it is another person has, then we must take heed to know that an unhealthy seed is growing in us.

Aside from the pride of Lucifer, scripture says he wanted to be like God and craved to be worshipped (Isaiah 14:12-15). For this reason, God cast him down the earth. Our God detests envy so much that He teaches us from His Word that whoever harbors envy is unwise, unspiritual, and demonic. James 3:15 True is this statement, for when we harbor envy, we become open to the devil's attack. We become vulnerable to other evil spirits such as pride, lust, and malice, and they begin to find expression in our lives.

As children of God, we must know that the devil is very subtle and can plant the seed of envy in our hearts. Just like Paul warned, "Take heed lest you fall (1 Corinthians 10:12,NKJV). We must, therefore, carefully examine our hearts daily to ensure we are not given to the devil's ploy. The moment you notice any trace of envy, you must be honest first with yourself, and then admit to God the wrong, asking the Lord for mercy. Sometimes, all we need do is to improve ourselves and work harder. Other times, we do not necessarily need what they have and in other cases, we must learn to understand that we are peculiarly made in God's image and likeness. Each of us has a separate gift and a separate calling. Find yours and don't envy others that have found theirs.

Envy separates us from God. It enslaves us with evil thoughts. Joseph's brothers' envy led to his being sold. Cain's envy led to him committing murder. Envy and hatred led the Pharisees and Sadducees to despise Jesus, for they not only felt He was attracting large crowds, but also that He taught with so much authority and performed many miracles which they could not.

Pray:

Yahweh, teach me to abhor envy; teach me rather to work on myself and improve myself. Help me discover my purpose and gifting that I may not envy others, and help me to walk in Your ways today, amen.

Further reading: Proverbs 14:30, James 3:16, Galatians 5:26, 1 Corinthians 13:4, Proverbs 23:17.

Ponder:

☐ What signs should I watch out for to ensure I'm not being envious of others?

☐ Has there ever been a time that you have been envious of someone?

☐ What is the repercussion of envy?

My reflection.

The thoughts that stood out to me are: DATE _____

Bible Devotional Guide Day 7:

Topic: **Failure**

Read: **Romans 8:28 NLT**

Key Verse:

"And we know that God causes everything to work together for the good of those who love God and are called according to his purpose for them."

Apply:

Failure is a word that can evoke feelings of shame, disappointment, or regret. It is often seen as a negative symbol of falling short of our expectations or our inability to succeed or achieve our goals. The truth is, we all have failed in certain things at some point in our lives. It could be a sales pitch, a team presentation, an exam, or a game. We easily become overwhelmed, discouraged, or depressed.

When faced with failure, it is not unusual to feel negative emotions - anger, disappointment etc., but what matters most is how we move on when faced with it.

Most people begin to question God and His purpose; some begin to doubt their ability, and some move into a state of denial and nonchalance. But what does God's Word have to say? James 1: 2-4 says that we should "count it all joy, my brothers, when you meet trials of various kinds, for you know that the testing of your faith produces steadfastness. And let steadfastness have its full effect, that you may be perfect and complete, lacking in nothing (ESV)." This verse reminds us that, as believers, we will most definitely encounter trials (failure), especially in cases where we have absolute faith in our ability. But we should see it as stepping stones towards growth and maturity.

Ultimately, when we experience failure, we have an opportunity to turn to God in prayer and seek His guidance. Through Christ, we are given the grace to overcome our shortcomings and rise above our mistakes. As Romans 8:28 says, God works for the good of those who love Him. This verse assures us that God can use our failures to fulfill His divine plan and bring about good for His people.

Let us not be discouraged by our failures, but rather see them as an opportunity to draw closer to God and trust in His unfailing love and grace. As we surrender our weaknesses, He will turn our failures into triumphs and transform us into the image of His Son.

Pray:

Jehovah, help me let go of the feeling that comes with failure. I know it is not Your will for fears to hold me back from fulfilling my purpose. Forgive me for not living in faith, and help me from this moment on to live with bold confidence in You. Lord, help me not compare myself to others around me. Amen.

Further reading: Philippians 4:13, Proverbs 24:16, Isaiah 41:10.

Ponder:

- ☐ Have you ever felt the sting of failure before?

- ☐ What is your greatest failure?

- ☐ Is it possible for a child of God to experience failure?

My reflection.

The thoughts that stood out to me are: DATE _____

Bible Devotional Guide Day 8:

Topic: Love

Read: Matt.22:34- 40 KJV

Key Verse:

"But when the Pharisees had heard that he had put the Sadducees to silence, they were gathered together. Then one of them, which was a lawyer, asked him a question, tempting him, and saying, Master, which is the great commandment in the law? Jesus said unto him, thou shalt love the Lord thy God with all thy heart, and with all thy soul, and with all thy mind. This is the first and great commandment. And the second is like unto it, thou shalt love thy neighbor as thyself. On these two commandments hang all the law and the prophets."

Apply:

Love is a great gift from God! It is a virtue filled with so many attributes. Love is one of the most commonly used words in our world today; yet, very few express its attributes; the larger number uses it as a word to express delight over a thing or to express a sexual desire to the opposite sex. The word *love* has been classified into types by various scholars, but the love that we are talking about is that which Jesus taught and that is, the love of the Father to us, our love for our God, and our love to our neighbor.

The Word of God speaks on true love which is the love of the Father towards us, His children, called the "Agape love." This love is unconditional (John 15:13 - Greater love has no one than this, that someone lay down his life for his friends). The Bible teaches us (John 3:16) that while we were yet sinners Christ died for us. Can you imagine such love? That Jesus the Son of God was beaten to disfiguration, yet those He laid down His life for hated Him – some even today?

Again, God is love; 1 John 4:8 says anyone who does not love does not know God, because God is love. This simply means anyone who does not know God cannot love! Love is patient, is kind, does not envy, does not parade itself, is not puffed up, does not behave rudely, etc. (I Corinthians 13:1-13, NKJV).

To love the Lord rightly, Jesus teaches us that we must love the Lord with all our heart, our soul, and our mind (Matthew 22:37, NLT). When we do this, we seek to know how to please the Lord in every way, to worship rightly, and obey all that He commands us to do. Also, Jesus teaches us to love our neighbor as ourselves. Our neighbor is not just the person living next door but whoever we find around us at any given moment in time (Luke 10:25-37). He also taught us to love our enemies (Luke 6:27-36). One of the best ways to express our love in these times is by sharing "The Good News" to all: Christ came to earth, died, resurrected, and is coming back to take those who love, believe in and have surrendered their lives to Him.

Pray:

Creator, thank You for Your saving grace, teach me today to love You more with all my heart, soul, and mind--to love my neighbor as I love myself. Give me the grace to tell the world about Your love by my conduct and by my speech.

Further reading: John 15:13, 1 John 4:7-8, Mark 12:30-31, Ephesians 5:2, Romans 13:10

Ponder:

☐   What is love?

☐   How should we show that we love our neighbor?

☐   What are some examples of showing love?

My reflection.

The thoughts that stood out to me are: DATE _____

_____

_____

_____

_____

_____

_____

_____

_____

_____

_____

_____

_____

_____

_____

_____

_____

_____

_____

_____

Bible Devotional Guide Day 9:

Topic: **Patience**

Read: **Hebrews 10:35-36 NLT**

Key Verse:

So, do not throw away this confident trust in the Lord. Remember the great reward it brings you! Patient endurance is what you need now, so that you will continue to do God's will. Then you will receive all that he has promised.

Apply:

Patience is the ability to bear difficulties or delays without becoming frustrated. Most of us would like to be more patient, but it's not always that simple. As we go through life, we encounter instances in which the answers to such concerns appear slow to arrive, and we frequently become weary and lose faith in their manifestation.

God's Word teaches us to wait even when it takes longer than intended (Habakkuk 2:3). Because when we wait on God until the end, He brings us His intended promises.

We should also learn to understand that our lives on earth vary and that everyone has an assigned period for his/her life based on God's plans for us. Impatience arises when we feel the need to have everything we want at the exact time we want it, and when it does not arrive at that time, we become impatient and fail to trust God.

When you exercise patience, you are simply expressing your faith in God and relying completely on Him (Proverbs 3:5-6), knowing that His plans for you are the best and will come to pass in His time.

Look at Abraham's life. We see a man who had faith and patience to wait for the Lord's given time, and God blessed him to the point that we also are partakers of Abraham's blessings to this day.

Today, remember to wait on God and trust the Holy Spirit to assist.

Pray:

Elohim, teach me to be patient in all things, remembering at all times that Your plans for me are distinct from those of my neighbors or my family. Help me lean totally on You and wait upon You for all my needs. Amen.

Further reading: Proverbs 15:18, Romans 8:25, Psalm 62:1.

Ponder:

☐ Have you ever yearned for anything so long that it seems unlikely that it will materialize?

☐ Why must we have patience?

☐ How do you exercise patience?

My reflection.

The thoughts that stood out to me are: DATE _____

La'Tosha M. Aikens

Topic: **Peace**

Read: **Matthew 8:23-26 MSG**

Key Verse:

"Then he got into the boat and his disciples followed him. Without warning a furious storm came up on the lake so that the wave swept over the boat. But Jesus was sleeping. The disciples went and woke him up saying "Lord save us! We are going to drown!" He replied," You of little faith, why are you afraid ... Peace I leave with you; my peace I give to you. Not as the world gives do I give to you. Let not your hearts be troubled, neither let them be afraid."

Apply:

A songwriter wrote a song which had this wording: Why worry when you can pray, trust in Jesus and He will lead the way; don't be a doubting Thomas. Just trust in all God's promises; so why worry when you can pray?

We sometimes experience a peaceful moment in our lives, but when life challenges rise, we fall back into worry, pressure, and in some cases, depression. This peace, therefore, as children of God, the devil stages war in our minds to prevent us from knowing God's will for each time over a matter and so he intentionally creates noise with distractions that makes us less discerning. We must learn to walk by The Spirit so that we may not gratify the desires of the flesh that are short-lived, because this is what most of us in today's world consider peace. But as children of God, the peace spoken about is a fruit of the Holy Spirit.

It takes FAITH to have this kind of peace. Like the proverb states, you'll have to lean not on your understanding (Proverbs 3:5). Without warning, some stormy situations such as loss of our source of income, worry about becoming successful, or even death may bring us to the point of panic. But God's Word teaches that your peace comes in the assurance of God's Word being spoken over our lives from even before we were formed. Focus on God's promises in His words and the peace of the Lord will flood your heart. Then you must understand that the battle or crisis is not yours but the Lord's (2 Chronicles 20:15).

Notice that the only thing Jesus said to His disciples was, "Ye of little faith." Likewise when Peter started sinking Jesus reached out for him and asked him "Why did you doubt" (Matthew 14:31)? God is speaking to us today, and in the stillness of your heart is saying, *Trust Me*, and in assurance according to His Word has given us the peace that we can only find in Him. Today, fix your gaze on Jesus, for He is the Lord of peace (Isaiah 26:3, 2 Thessalonians 3:16).

Pray:

Father, in You I rest today. Give me Your peace that supersedes all human understanding especially as I walk in faith today. Help me to lean on You, take my gaze away from anxiety and place it assuredly on You, Jesus. Amen.

Further reading: Isaiah 26:3, Philippians 4:7, Romans 12:18, Psalm 29:11, Matthew 5:9, Colossians 3:15.

Ponder:

☐ How can I sustain peace at all times even amid crisis?

☐ What should I do when I begin to panic and worry about things?

☐ What am I most worried about now?

My reflection.

The thoughts that stood out to me are: Date

Bible Devotional Guide Day 11:

Topic: Happiness

Read: Psalm 37:4 KJV

Key Verse:

"Delight thyself also in the LORD, and he shall give thee the desires of thine heart."

Apply:

There is an endless pursuit of happiness humankind is engaged in. It's what fuels the good, bad, and terrible things we see around us. Does God want us to be happy? Yes! But that kind of happiness is not the kind the world pursues.

The world seeks happiness as an end with self-satisfaction at its center. But it shall not be so with you. The Lord is to be your delight. Our happiness is centered on God and God alone. Though other things may make us happy, it should be because they help us serve the purposes of God.

When your happiness is not centered on earthly things, it can help you avoid making a god out of them. That is how you'll be able to remain joyful if those things are taken away. Delight in God! Let Him be the whole essence of joy and happiness to you.

The Bible says, "Delight thyself in the Lord" (Psalm 37:4). This means feeding your delight with the knowledge of Jesus Christ through constant studying of the Word, praying, meditating, worshipping, and serving in the house of the Lord, as well as sharing the love of Christ with people.

You don't need to seek any form of acceptance to live in happiness. Knowing that God has wiped clean your record of sin makes you live above sadness, guilt, shame, and doubt (Romans 4:8). God loves you, and He will do everything to make you happy. Rest on His unfailing love and watch how you will blossom in happiness.

Pray:

Sweet Jesus, help me make You my greatest delight. Help me hold loosely to all that is not eternal. Fill my heart with joy and happiness. Take away sorrows, pain, guilt, shame, and doubt from my heart today. Let me experience genuine happiness that only You can give. Amen.

Further reading: Proverbs 15:13, Romans 15:13, Ecclesiastes 2:26, Psalm 144:15.

Ponder:

☐ What makes the difference between a believer's desire to be happy and that of an unbeliever?

☐ What has the quest for happiness made you become?

☐ How do I find happiness within?

My reflection.

The thoughts that stood out to me are: DATE _____

Bible Devotional Guide Day 12:

Topic: Healing

Read: Isaiah 57:18-19 NIV

Key Verse:

I have seen their ways, but I will heal them; I will guide them and restore comfort to Israel's mourners, creating praise on their lips. Peace, peace, to those far and near," says the LORD. "And I will heal them."

Apply:

When it comes to healing, most of us put off starting a healthy lifestyle until we are sick. In the face of a medical emergency, we are then at the mercy of science.

Even though the majority of the world is believers of Christ, few people know how to obtain immediate healing from God. In every church and home, Divine Healing should be understood and practiced. This is a reassuring phrase offered by Jesus, "Come to me, all you who are weary and burdened, and I will give you rest" (Matthew 11:28, NIV).

A lot of people are faced with the problem of utilizing this divine healing power. Lack of faith and ignorance could hinder the use of the power of healing that resides within us. All we have to do to receive healing is to genuinely "believe." This power is ours to use; we can say to a "fever" to release its hold over our body, and it would stop. Whatever kind of healing you desire, be it emotional, mental, financial, relationship, or health-wise, God is willing to heal you completely and set you free today.

As simple as the act of believing is, it can be overwhelming especially when we have doubt and signs of the sickness still looming around. The best way to overcome this is to see times of healing as also great opportunities to exercise your faith by declaring the Word of God as it concerns healing. Vehemently refuse to stay down, go about your routine in the faith that knowing you're being totally healed. You will be healed.

Pray:

Healer, help me to keep my focus on You when the pain and hurt are overwhelming. Help me be faithful and see the good and blessings surrounding me. Please strengthen my mind, heart, and body, and heal me today. In Your name I pray, amen.

Further reading: James 5:14-15, Isaiah 53:4-5, Jeremiah 30:17; 33:6, Psalm 41:3.

Ponder:

- ☐ Is it always God's will to heal?

- ☐ How can I receive healing?

- ☐ What are you trusting God to heal in your life currently?

My reflection.

The thoughts that stood out to me are: DATE _____

La'Tosha M. Aikens

Bible Devotional Guide Day 13:

Topic: Compassion

Read: Ephesians 4:32 ESV

Key Verse:

"Be kind to one another, tenderhearted, forgiving one another, as God in Christ forgave you."

Apply:

Compassion is the capacity to sympathize with someone's suffering, feeling it and desiring to assist. It is to see someone's pain and sorrow and desire to help lift them up. Compassionate actions can be as simple as offering sincere words of kindness and understanding or as time-consuming and costly as offering the provision of tangible needs.

God is compassionate. At the core of the Gospel is the story of God's compassion for us and His offer of mercy and grace through His Son Jesus. He loves the brokenhearted and those suffering from oppression, looking down on them, knowing all the details of their circuitous paths to the bottom, and choosing to faithfully bring freedom and healing.

It is therefore critical for believers to imitate God's compassion and mercy. We must resist the urge to end our interaction and relationship with those that have hurt us. Philippians 2:3-4 (NIV) says, "Do nothing from selfish ambition or conceit, but in humility count others more significant than yourselves. Let each of you look not only to his interests but also to the interests of others."

Remember the Parable of the Good Samaritan? In Luke 10:25-37, Jesus shared this story to highlight the essence of compassion. Despite cultural and societal differences, the Samaritan chose to care for and help a stranger in need. It reminds us that compassion breaks down barriers and calls us to love beyond our comfort zones.

We must faithfully and intentionally practice mercy, identifying with those in distress and sorrow, recognizing our brokenness and dependence on a faithful God.

Pray:

Jehovah Nissi, You are great to be praised! You are loving and merciful, and You have shown us great compassion. Help us to be compassionate and merciful to those around us, to look out for the interests of others, and to show mercy and grace just as You have done for us. Amen.

Further reading: Matthew 9:36; Luke 10:33-34; Romans 9:15; Colossians 3:12-14; James 3:17; Matthew 5:7.

Ponder:

☐ What does it really mean to be compassionate?

☐ How does it look practically in our day-to-day lives?

☐ What do we need to remember if we want to grow in compassion?

My reflection.

The thoughts that stood out to me are: DATE _____

Topic: **Wisdom**

Read: **Proverbs 4:7 ESV**

Key Verse:

"The beginning of wisdom is this: Get wisdom, and whatever you get, get insight."

Apply:

Wisdom is a powerful thing. It's having knowledge and discernment to make the right decisions to guide us in our lives. We are all familiar with the phrase "ignorance is bliss." But when it comes to being a believer, ignorance is anything but bliss! Having wisdom will help us to understand the plans and purposes God has for our lives. When we seek true wisdom from the Lord, He will provide it. James 1:5 says, "If any of you lacks wisdom, let him ask God, who gives generously to all without reproach, and it will be given him" (NKJV). This is such an amazing promise that God gives to us. He longs for us to grow into the people He knows we can be – wise beyond our years, full of insights, and equipped to make the right decisions.

However, wisdom does not come without effort. We must take an active part in gaining knowledge of God's word and what it says about various aspects of life. We must start first by simply studying and reading what the Bible has to say about wisdom and then applying it in our own lives (Proverbs 18:15). explains that "an intelligent heart acquires knowledge, and the ear of the wise seeks knowledge" (ESV). As believers, we must be diligent in studying and teaching humility, which is a big part of wisdom.

This way, we can learn from the mistakes of our predecessors and be able to properly address any situation life throws our way. If we desire wisdom, then we must do the hard work of seeking it out, studying it, and applying it to our lives. We will be blessed with the rewards that come along with wisdom.

Wisdom leads to contentment, success, and a deeper understanding of God's grace and mercy. Proverbs 3:13-15 tells us that "blessed are those who find wisdom, those who gain understanding, for she is more profitable than silver and yields better returns than gold. She is more precious than rubies; nothing you desire can compare with her" (NIV).

Pray:

El Roi, we thank You for the promise that You give to us; that if we seek understanding and wisdom, You will provide it for us. Help us to be diligent in studying and applying the knowledge of Your Word to our lives. Fill us with Your Spirit of wisdom so that we may continue to walk in Your light. All this we ask in Jesus' name, Amen.

Further reading: Psalm 107: 43, Proverbs 2: 1-9, James 1:5, Proverbs 16:20, Proverbs 8:11, Luke 2:52.

Ponder:

- ☐ What is true wisdom? Does everyone have access to it?

- ☐ What is the importance of wisdom in the life of a believer?

- ☐ What has wisdom protected you from?

My reflection.

The thoughts that stood out to me are: DATE _____

_____

_____

_____

_____

_____

_____

_____

_____

_____

_____

_____

_____

_____

_____

La'Tosha M. Aikens

Bible Devotional Guide Day 15:

Topic: **Unity**

Read: **Ephesians 4:3 NIV**

Key Verse:

"Make every effort to keep the unity of the Spirit through the bond of peace."

Apply:

Living in unity is essential for believers to ensure we're walking in harmony with God's will. Unity among believers is a tool to be used, not just to be talked about. When we strive to be united, it reflects the love of Christ to the rest of the world and brings us closer to Him as well. Psalm 133:1 reminds us, "How good and pleasant it is when God's people live together in unity"(NIV)! Living in unity means we must lay aside our differences and come together in agreement. This is not easy; it takes a lot of effort on our part to do this. We must make an effort to reach out and extend love to others - even those who may not agree with us. Christ teaches us that loving one another is the greatest act of unity and that by doing so, we can honor God and His Word.

Living in unity can create a sense of security and comfort for us and those around us. We should look for ways to show we respect and value others, even if we disagree. This could be an inviting smile, a kind word, or offering assistance when we can. This can help bring an atmosphere of unity and peace.

We must also be careful to make sure we are committing our efforts to building up unity and not tearing it down. We should work to edify one another and discourage jealousy and strife in our relationships. Open communication in a spirit of humility and love is essential for unity.

Finally, as with everything in life, prayer is key. We must be in prayer daily, asking God to guide our conversations and cultivate a spirit of unity among us. We can also pray for others who may be going through a difficult place in their lives and may need the love and support of others to get through it.

Pray:

Jehovah Tsidkenu, thank You for uniting us in Your love. Help us to strive to live in unity, seeing each other the way You see us – beyond our differences. Fill us with Your Spirit, so that we can reach out and extend a spirit of love and acceptance to our brothers and sisters in Christ. Grant us the ability to forgive and to love each other in the same way You love us. In Jesus' wonderful name, amen.

Further reading: Psalm 133:1, Philippians 2:1-4, Romans 12:16, Colossians 3:14-17.

Ponder:

- ☐ What does it mean to live in unity?

- ☐ Is it possible to live in unity with others, even when we may disagree?

- ☐ How can we cultivate an atmosphere of unity and peace even when times are tough?

My reflection.

The thoughts that stood out to me are: DATE _____

_____

_____

_____

_____

_____

_____

_____

_____

_____

_____

_____

_____

_____

_____

_____

_____

_____

Bible Devotional Guide Day 16:

Topic: Kindness

Read: Luke 19:1-9 KJV

Key Verse:

8-Meanwhile, Zacchaeus stood before the Lord and said, "I will give half my wealth to the poor, Lord, and if I have cheated people on their taxes, I will give them back four times as much!" Jesus responded, "Salvation has come to this home today, for this man has shown himself to be a true son of Abraham.

Apply:

Being kind is an act of selflessness. It is an act of making others happy without any specific reasons. Kindness is a fruit of the Holy Spirit that enables you to love and give selflessly to others without expecting a favor in return. Showing kindness is not a seasonal trait but a virtue one should have. It is soothing to know that the Holy Spirit enables us to express kindness better to others.

Kindness to others extends beyond purchasing gifts and providing assistance, no matter how vital these things are. Giving a warm smile or hug to a discouraged friend or family, is an act of kindness, as is speaking favorably of others, checking in on friends, thanking the waiter or even thanking the trash collector. What matters most is that you leave an imprint of love in that person's heart, making them feel more valued and valuable. When we exhibit compassion to others, we usually teach them to show kindness to others as well.

An example from scripture is Jesus' gesture of compassion to Zacchaeus, which later brought redemption to Zacchaeus. Jesus, rather than reprimanding him for duping people or speaking badly of him, was gracious enough to pay him a visit and lunch with him. This act led

Zacchaeus to repentance and compelled him to repay all he had cheated. This shows that being kind changes the lives of those who receive it in most cases. Don't wait for someone to show you an act of kindness before you reciprocate. The Word of God has instructed us to live out this character daily.

Pray:

Jehovah Machsi, please teach me to show kindness to everyone around me. Help me by Your Spirit to do this without expecting anything in return that people will see You in all that I do. Amen.

Further reading: Romans 12:8, Proverbs 15:4, Ephesians 4:32

Ponder:

☐ When is it best to show acts of kindness to others?

☐ How have you shown acts of kindness lately?

☐ Must I give gifts or render services to be considered kind?

My reflection.

The thoughts that stood out to me are: DATE

La'Tosha M. Aikens

Bible Devotional Guide Day 17:

Topic: Self-Control

Read: Proverbs 25:28 NLT

Key Verse:

"A person without self-control is like a city with broken-down walls."

Apply:

The ability to refrain oneself from doing something is termed "self-control." It could be refraining from hurting individuals who have injured you, thinking negative thoughts, or giving in to temptations that lead to wrongdoing.

The Bible teaches us today that self-control is a fruit of the Holy Spirit; in other words, we don't have the power to withstand the pressures of this world on our own, but the Holy Spirit helps us wield our will in line with God's desire for us.

The Bible compares someone who lacks self-control to a city with shattered walls; in other words, when you lack self-control, you become subject to the devil's attacks because he gains control over your thoughts and actions. We become slaves to sin if we lack self-control (Romans 6:16). Lack of self-control can cause us to miss God's promises. For example, Moses could not enter the Promised Land due to a lack of self-control and anger (Deuteronomy 32:51-52).

When we submit our will to God's will, we become subject to His Spirit, which helps us control ourselves and keeps us from doing things that are out of our control or the wrong things. After forty days and nights of fasting, Jesus was tempted by the devil, but he overcame him with the help of the Holy Spirit and the word of God - resisting the devil vehemently (Matthew 4:1).

We cannot exercise self-control over things around us through our own will and power, but we can gain self-control by trusting and depending on God (Proverbs 3:5-6), being guided by the Spirit (Galatians 5:16), and walking in love (Galatians 5:13-14). When we exercise self-control, we are living following God's Word.

Pray:

Holy Father, I cannot exhibit self-control on my own. I've learned by Your Word today that You can help me with Your Spirit. I, therefore, submit my will to Yours, Lord, and I ask that by Your grace I'll live a life just like Christ's and that through my self-control others may see Jesus in my life. Amen.

Further reading: 1 Corinthians 7:5, 1 Timothy 1:7, Titus 2:6.

Ponder:

☐ Have you ever felt so pushed that you were tempted to fight back or give in to pressures from other people or any situation?

☐ Is it possible for a child of God to have self-control?

☐ How do you practice self-control?

My reflection.

The thoughts that stood out to me are: DATE _____

_____

_____

_____

_____

_____

_____

_____

_____

_____

_____

_____

_____

_____

_____

_____

_____

_____

La'Tosha M. Aikens

Bible Devotional Guide Day 18:

Topic: **Mercy**

Read: **Micah 6:8 NIV**

Key Verse:

"He has shown you, O mortal, what is good. And what does the Lord require of you? To act justly and to love mercy and to walk humbly with your God."

Apply:

Mercy is essential in our relationships. It allows us to forgive those who have wronged us and release the burden of bitterness. As followers of Christ, we are called to forgive as we have been forgiven (Colossians 3:13). By extending mercy, we open the door for healing and restoration in our relationships.

Mercy breaks the cycle of judgment and condemnation. It reminds us that we are all flawed and in need of God's grace. When we show mercy to others, we acknowledge our own need for mercy and create an environment of acceptance and understanding. Instead of passing judgment, we become agents of reconciliation and hope. When we choose to be merciful, we align ourselves with God's heart. It softens our hearts and helps us cultivate empathy, compassion, and humility.

In a world filled with conflict and division, being a peacemaker is an act of mercy. Strive to promote peace in your relationships, communities, and even in broader society. Seek reconciliation, bridge gaps, and strive to bring people together in love and understanding.

The importance of believers being merciful cannot be overstated. Mercy reflects the heart of God and demonstrates our gratitude for the mercy we have received from Him. It is through acts of mercy that we become vessels of His love and grace in the world.

When we extend mercy, we not only bless others, but also experience the transformative power of God's mercy in our own lives. As we show mercy, we open ourselves up to receiving mercy from God and others. It is a reciprocal relationship where mercy begets mercy.

Pray:

Lord Master, thank You for Your abundant mercy that You have shown to us through Jesus Christ. Help us to understand the depth of Your mercy and to extend it to others. Soften our hearts and give us the strength to forgive and show compassion even when it is difficult. May Your mercy flow through us and bring healing to our relationships and communities. In Jesus' name, amen.

Further reading: Psalm 103:8, Ephesians 2:4-5, James 2:13, Luke 6:36, Colossians 3:12, Micah 6:8, Luke 10:33-37.

Ponder:

- ☐ How does this verse challenge your understanding of mercy?

- ☐ Name a time God has shown mercy to you?

- ☐ And how does God's mercy towards you impact your response to others?

My reflection.

The thoughts that stood out to me are: DATE

Bible Devotional Guide Day 19:

Topic: Chosen

Read: Deuteronomy 7:6-8 KJV

Key Verse:

The LORD thy God hath chosen thee to be a special people unto himself... The LORD did not set his love upon you, nor choose you because ye were more in number than any people... But because the LORD loved you..."

Apply:

Imagine a believer thinking they were saved because they were educated and the kingdom had things to gain from an educated saint. Oftentimes, we tie God's election to human qualification, but the truth is, it's because of God's love.

It is good to meditate on divine election; it drives us to worship. Knowing that God chose us while we were still rebels, when there was nothing good in us is a blessing. If He had left us to ourselves, we would have never chosen first. But because of His love, He chose us to be a special possession unto Him. This should keep you humble and in perpetual worship.

God chose you for a reason, a holy people to show forth the glory of a holy God. Your life should be like billboards displaying the beauties and glories of God. Do this by walking in a manner worthy of your calling and living the fullness of life in Christ. Consider your life and seek that every aspect of it becomes a showroom for God's glory in the dark and dying world.

The Bible also says in 1 Peter 2:9, "*But you are not like that, for you are a chosen people. You are royal priests, a holy nation, God's very own possession. As a result, you can show others the goodness of God, for he called you out of the darkness into his wonderful light"* (NLT). It is a privilege to be chosen by God and an honor to show others the goodness of God. Living in this consciousness that you're chosen by God, should inspire you to live up to His expectations.

Pray:

El Elyon, who am I that Your love reached out for me in the mud of sin and death? Thank You for choosing me. Lord, as I live my life every day help me so that every part of it points to Your glory and grace. Amen.

Further reading: Ephesians 1:4-5, John 15:16, Romans 8:29, 2 Thessalonians 2:13

Ponder:

☐ What do you think are the basics for God's election (God choosing us)?

☐ Have you ever felt that you weren't chosen by God?

☐ There should be a purpose for God's choosing us, have you considered it and are you living up to it?

My reflection.

The thoughts that stood out to me are: DATE _____

Topic: **Faithfulness**

Read: **Matthew 25:21 ESV**

Key Verse:

"His master said to him, 'Well done, good and faithful servant. You have been faithful over a little; I will set you over much. Enter into the joy of your master."

Apply:

Faithfulness is all about steadfastness, loyalty, and reliability. When we talk about faithfulness, it encompasses various aspects of our lives. First and foremost, it's about being faithful in our relationship with God. This means staying committed to Him, seeking Him wholeheartedly, and walking in obedience to His Word. It involves nurturing a consistent prayer life and cultivating intimacy with Him. Through faithfulness, we show our love and devotion to our Heavenly Father.

But faithfulness doesn't stop there. It also extends to our relationships with others. Being faithful means being a trustworthy and dependable friend, family member, and neighbor. It means honoring our commitments, keeping our promises, and being there for others when they need us. Our faithfulness in relationships reflects the faithfulness of God, showing others His love through our actions.

Additionally, faithfulness is vital in how we handle the responsibilities and resources entrusted to us. Whether it's our work, finances, talents, or time, faithfulness calls us to be diligent and responsible stewards. When we are faithful in managing what God has given us, we demonstrate gratitude and honor Him as the ultimate Provider.

So, why is it important for believers to be faithful? Well, faithfulness is a reflection of our character as followers of Christ. It sets us apart in a world that often values convenience and self-interest. Our faithfulness testifies to the unchanging nature of God and His faithfulness toward us. It strengthens our witness to others, showing them the transformative power of the Gospel in our lives.

Faithfulness opens the door to greater blessings and rewards from God. As we see in the parable, the servant's faithfulness resulted in being entrusted with more. When we are faithful in the "little" things, God entrusts us with greater opportunities and responsibilities. Our faithfulness positions us to experience the joy and fulfillment of living out God's purpose for our lives.

Pray:

El Olam, thank You for Your unwavering faithfulness towards me. Help me to grow in faithfulness in every area of my life. Grant me the strength and perseverance to remain faithful in my relationship with You, in my interactions with others, and my responsibilities and stewardship. May my faithfulness bring glory to Your name and draw others to You. In Jesus' name, amen.

Further reading: 2 Corinthians 4:2, Galatians 5:22, Revelation 2:10, 1 Peter 4:19, Luke 4:42-44, Matthew 24:45-47.

Ponder:

- ☐ What does it mean to be faithful?

- ☐ How does faithfulness impact our relationship with God?

- ☐ Why is it essential for believers to exhibit faithfulness?

My reflection.

The thoughts that stood out to me are: DATE _____

_____

_____

_____

_____

_____

_____

_____

_____

_____

_____

_____

_____

_____

_____

La'Tosha M. Aikens

Bible Devotional Guide Day 21:

Topic: **Honor**

Read: **Philippians 2:3-11**

Key Verse:

"Let this mind be in you, which was also in Christ Jesus: Who, being in the form of God, thought it not robbery to be equal with God: But made himself of no reputation, and took upon him the form of a servant, and was made in the likeness of men: And being found in fashion as a man, he humbled himself, and became obedient unto death, even the death of the cross."

Apply:

Honor is not merely a concept but a reflection of our hearts and actions. Our world today talks about and applauds putting oneself first above all, which makes the idea of honor sound so outdated. But we can agree that honor is a biblical principle. It's a virtue that highlights respect, esteem, and admiration toward others, especially those who have served and contributed to society in various ways. As believers, we are called to honor others, including God, our parents, our leaders, our spouses, and even our enemies.

Honor begins with recognizing the intrinsic worth of others, while we may disagree with their decisions and policy. It involves treating people with respect, dignity, and kindness, regardless of their position, age, or background. Perhaps the most profound example of honor is found in Jesus Christ Himself. Philippians 2:6 reminds us that although Jesus was equal with God, He humbled Himself and became a servant, even to the point of death on the cross. This act of sacrificial love and honor demonstrated Christ's willingness to put others first.

To honor God in our daily lives means to acknowledge His presence in our lives and to live according to His teachings and commands. It involves recognizing God as the ultimate authority and prioritizing His will above our desires. Honoring God can manifest in various ways, such as through prayer and worship, serving others, and obeying His commands.

Ultimately, honoring God should be a daily commitment because as we honor God, He blesses us in ways we cannot imagine, and we can bless those around us as well. Let us strive to honor God in all that we do.

Pray:

King of Glory, thank You for reminding us of the importance of honor in our lives. Help us to cultivate a heart that honors You and others. Teach us to value and respect those around us, including our parents, authority figures, and all whom You have placed in our lives, and guide our steps to honor You through our thoughts, words, and actions. Amen.

Further reading: Exodus 20:12, Proverbs 3:9, Romans 12:10, 1 Timothy 5:17

Ponder:

☐ What does it mean to honor God?

☐ Has there ever been a time where you did not honor God?

☐ How can we cultivate a heart of honor in our daily lives?

My reflection.

The thoughts that stood out to me are: DATE _____

Topic: **Prayer**

Read: **Philippians 4:6-7 NLT**

Key Verse:

Don't worry about anything; instead, pray about everything. Tell God what you need, and thank him for all he has done. Then you will experience God's peace, which exceeds anything we can understand. His peace will guard your hearts and minds as you live in Christ Jesus.

Apply:

Everyone has prayed at some point in their lives; you don't need to be religious to do so. "Oh, God! Let the issue be resolved once more." This is a brief and straightforward statement that is, nevertheless, powerful enough to be called "a prayer." You might have prayed as a result of certain circumstances. But, do you understand the mystery that surrounds a straightforward prayer? Prayer is a simple act of communication between you and God; it brings us in touch with God and the people around us.

Whenever we pray, we offer every situation to God. We let God in on what and how we feel about ourselves, our situation, and the people around us. He allows His peace to guard our hearts and minds, just as we patiently wait to get our answers.

A lot of people find it difficult to pray or communicate with God. Ignorance and a feeling of doubt make it difficult to keep a constant prayer life. We should understand that it is God's will for us to pray, and as we pray, God listens, and He most definitely answers. Since it is God's will that we pray, you might ask, "How often should I pray?"

God's words gave us insights into how powerful and efficient the prayer of one righteous person is. If you know, as a righteous person, the potency of your prayer, saying it in situations as simple as locating a lost item should explain how often we can pray. There is no such thing as over-praying. As long as we pray, we obey God's will.

Pray:

Alpha and Omega, I understand Your will for me in the place of prayer, and I humbly ask that You teach me to harness the power of prayer and help me develop and find a will to communicate with You constantly, even in simple things. Reveal to me the power that comes from praying while trusting that you listen. In Jesus' name, amen!

Further reading: James 5:16, Matthew 6:6, Jeremiah 29:12, 1 Thessalonians 5:16-18, Mark 11:24, Luke 18:1, Ephesians 6:18

Ponder:

☐ Why do most people find it difficult to pray constantly?

☐ What prayer are you seeking God to answer now?

☐ Why is it so important that I pray?

My reflection.

The thoughts that stood out to me are: DATE _____

_____

_____

_____

_____

_____

_____

_____

_____

_____

_____

_____

_____

_____

_____

_____

_____

_____

_____

La'Tosha M. Aikens

Bible Devotional Guide Day 23:

Topic: Witness

Read: Acts 1:8 NIV

Key Verse:

"But you will receive power when the Holy Spirit comes upon you, and you will be my witnesses in Jerusalem, in all Judea and Samaria, and to the ends of the earth."

Apply:

Witnessing is not merely sharing our faith; it is a calling, a divine commission given to us by God Himself. As believers, we are called to be His witnesses, empowered by the Holy Spirit to share the love and truth of the Gospel with those around us. This is not an option or an occasional task, but a vital part of our Christian journey.

We have been entrusted with a sacred responsibility to proclaim the Good News of salvation to all people, starting from our immediate surroundings and extending to the ends of the earth. Witnessing is an expression of our faith and obedience to God's command. When we embrace our role as witnesses, we not only impact the lives of others, but also experience a transformation ourselves. Witnessing is an avenue for personal growth and spiritual maturity.

But it's not just about duty or obligation. Witnessing is an expression of our faith. It's a way of saying, "I believe in the power of the Gospel, and I want others to experience it, too." We have seen lives transformed, chains broken, and hope restored through the message of Jesus Christ. How can we keep that to ourselves? It's like having the best news in the world and wanting to shout it from the rooftops!

Do you know what's even more exciting? Witnessing is not just for the benefit of others—it's for our growth, too. When we share our faith, it deepens our understanding of God's Word and challenges us to live out what we believe. It's a journey of growth and discipleship, where we learn to rely on God's guidance and trust in His faithfulness.

Think about the world we live in today. It's filled with pain, brokenness, and despair. As believers, we have the incredible privilege of offering a message of hope. We get to be the light in the darkness, the ones who bring comfort, encouragement, and the promise of a better tomorrow. It's an honor and a responsibility we shouldn't take lightly.

Pray:

Gracious Father, thank You for calling us to be Your witnesses. We acknowledge that we cannot fulfill this calling in our own strength. Use us as instruments of Your grace and love, so that many may come to know You and experience the joy of salvation. Amen.

Further reading: Matthew 28:19-20, Romans 1:16, Romans 10:14-15, Acts 1:8, Mark 16:15, 1 Peter 3:15.

Ponder:

☐ What is the significance of being a witness?

☐ Do you often think witnessing is for a selected few?

☐ How do you witness the goodness of God to others?

My reflection.

The thoughts that stood out to me are: DATE _____

_____

_____

_____

_____

_____

_____

_____

_____

_____

_____

_____

_____

_____

_____

_____

Bible Devotional Guide Day 24:

Topic: **Worship**

Read: **Psalm 95:6-7 KJV**

Key Verse:

"Come, let us bow down in worship, let us kneel before the LORD our Maker; for he is our God and we are the people of his pasture, the flock under his care."

Apply:

Worship is an expression of devotion and obedience to God. It is an expression of how great and mighty He is in the lives of the people He created. God wants His people to remember who He is and that He is worthy of our love and adoration.

Worship is often seen as an event or activity held in the presence of God on a certain day, in a certain place, with certain words and actions. While this is true, it is not the only way to engage in worship. Worship is a lifestyle, a 24/7 call to acknowledge, glorify, and thank God in all things.

We honor God and seek to obey His commands each day, not just on Sunday. Effective worship requires that we come to God with humble hearts. We are called to approach Him with awe and adoration and reverently lift our voices and spiritual hearts in the glorification of the King of kings.

Worship can be experienced in individuals, families, and the gathered assembly of the church. It allows its participants to center themselves around the One who alone is deserving of our highest praise. Worship is about declaring our dependence on God and affirming His power and greatness as we offer ourselves to Him. It is a posture of surrender, gratitude, and devotion that draws us closer to the Father.

As believers, we are called to live a life of worship to God. We honor Him with our bowed heads, our bent knees, and our surrendered hearts. Every action in life should be an act of worship—one that honors God and His truth. We are to live our lives for His service so that even when we are engaging in the activities of our daily lives, we are doing so with purpose and worship.

Pray:

Prince of Peace, thank You for the opportunity to worship You. Thank You for Your Word that teaches us about proper worship and helps shape our worshipful attitude. Help us to bring You our devotional offering of love, faithfulness, and obedience as we surrender ourselves fully to You. May our hearts continually be open to You and may our worship honor You in everything we do. In Jesus' name, amen.

Further reading: Psalm 97:7, Isaiah 12:1-6, Isaiah 6:1-8, Matthew 4:10, Luke 4:1-8.

Ponder:

☐ What does it mean to worship God?

☐ What should our attitude be when we approach God in worship?

☐ How can we make our worship pleasing to the Lord?

My reflection.

The thoughts that stood out to me are: DATE _____

_____

_____

_____

_____

_____

_____

_____

_____

_____

_____

_____

_____

_____

_____

_____

_____

_____

Bible Devotional Guide Day 25:

Topic: Grief

Read: 1 Thessalonians 4:13 ESV

Key Verse:

But we do not want you to be uninformed, brothers, about those who are asleep, that you may not grieve as others do who have no hope.

Apply:

The fall of humanity has given grief a front-row seat in creation, and not even believers can escape it. From the death of loved ones to the pain of persecution and suffering, we are met by this unpleasant visitor periodically. But we can't pass through this bridge of grief like the unsaved.

The Bible admonishes us to endure suffering by looking forward to our hope. Like Jesus, pass through grief looking towards the joy set before you, of the age to come where grief and its effect have no place. This High Priest (Jesus) understands what it means to be sorrowful. Forbear knowing He loves you and is with you even in the fire of grief.

There could be gold in grief, knowing that suffering is one of God's systems of virtue installation. The bitter taste can have alongside the sweet fruits of righteousness in your life. Through the season of grief, keep your eyes on Jesus! Matthew 5:4 (NKJV) says" *Blessed are those who mourn, For they shall be comforted." When we mourn over our sins in repentance and sincerity, God blesses us with comfort.*

In times of grief, turn to God as your ultimate source of comfort. Pour out your heart to Him, knowing that He understands your pain. Draw near to Him through prayer, reading His Word, and seeking His presence. Allow His love and peace to envelop you in your moments of sorrow.

Our faith in Jesus Christ gives us hope in the face of grief. We have the assurance that one day, all pain and sorrow will be replaced with joy and eternal life. Fix your eyes on the hope of the resurrection, knowing that God will redeem our suffering and bring beauty from ashes.

Pray:

El Chay, You know my frame. You see my scars. I cast this burden of grief before You. Fill me with Your joy. Lord, comfort me in this trying time, bring peace and comfort to my family and everyone believing You today for it. Take away grief and fill us with your exceeding joy. Amen.

Further reading: John 16:20, 33, Romans 8:18, Matthew 11:28-30.

Ponder:

☐ What effect has grief had on your faith and life in general?

☐ How did you navigate grief?

☐ What provision does the Christian worldview have to handle the problem of grief?

My reflection.

The thoughts that stood out to me are: DATE

_____

_____

_____

_____

_____

_____

_____

_____

_____

_____

_____

_____

_____

_____

_____

Bible Devotional Guide Day 26:

Topic: **Repentance**

Read: **1 John 1:9 NLT**

Key Verse:

But if we confess our sins to him, he is faithful and just to forgive us our sins and to cleanse us from all wickedness.

Apply:

Sometimes, we find ourselves falling short of God's perfect plan for our lives. At some point, we miss the mark, make a wrong decision, or choose a sinful path. But the beauty of God's love is we have been given a way to return to Him. That way is through repentance. Repentance is sincere remorse or regret for our sins or wrongdoings, accompanied by a commitment to change the behavior that led to those actions. It involves turning from our sin, confessing it to God, and asking for forgiveness. It is a complete turnaround from our sinful nature to a nature that seeks to please God.

When we repent, we acknowledge our wrongdoings and ask for forgiveness. This act of humility allows us to receive God's grace and mercy. We can see a perfect model of Repentance in the story of The Prodigal Son in Luke 15. The prodigal son realized and acknowledged his mistakes before deciding to return to his father. He confessed his wrongdoing, and he was welcomed back with open arms. Repentance always requires humility. The good news that comes with deciding to repent is that God is loving and merciful. He is always ready to forgive us when we come to Him with a repentant heart..."If we confess our sins, he is faithful and just to forgive us our sins and to cleanse us from all unrighteousness" (1 John 1:9 NIV). This is a powerful promise that gives us hope and reassurance. When we repent, God not only forgives us, but also He also cleanses us from the guilt of sin.

God is not interested in a superficial apology or mere lip service. He desires genuine remorse, a willingness to make amends, and a commitment to live righteously going forward. if we want to grow in our faith and become more like Christ, genuine repentance is necessary.

So today, let us examine our hearts and ask God to reveal any areas of sin in our lives. Let us have the humility to admit our mistakes and the courage to turn away from them. And let us remember that when we repent, we open ourselves up to the abundant grace and mercy of our loving Father in heaven.

Pray:

Chief Shephard, we acknowledge our sinfulness and our need for repentance. We confess our sins to You and ask for Your forgiveness. Renew our hearts and minds, and transform us into the people You want us to be. Help us to live a life of obedience to You and glorify Your name. In Jesus' name, we pray, amen.

Further reading: Acts 3:19, 2 Corinthians 7:9-10, 2 Peter 3:9

Ponder:

☐ Do you ever think it is impossible to turn back from so many wrongdoings?

☐ How can you tell if you genuinely want to turn a new leaf?

☐ Do you believe when you repent God forgives you instantly?

My reflection.

The thoughts that stood out to me are: DATE

La'Tosha M. Aikens

Bible Devotional Guide Day 27:

Topic: Fear

Read: Philippians 4:6-7 ESV

Key Verse:

"Do not be anxious about anything, but in everything by prayer and supplication with thanksgiving let your requests be made known to God. And the peace of God, which surpasses all understanding, will guard your hearts and your minds in Christ Jesus."

Apply:

Fear has a natural tendency to consume our minds if we let it. We will start to anticipate all the terrible outcomes of our current life situations until fear overtakes us. But what does the Bible say about fear? When we turn to scripture, we find that fear does not come from God. In 2 Timothy 1:7, Paul writes, "For God has not given us a spirit of fear but of power and love and self-control" (ESV). In other words, when fear creeps into our lives, it is not from God, but very likely from the enemy.

Therefore, the Bible encourages us to drive out fear and instead, fix our minds on things that are pure, true, honorable, just, lovely, and commendable (Philippians 4:8).

The Bible not only reminds us that fear is not from God, but it also encourages us to live in faith, not fear. It assures us that we can overcome the fear in our lives by trusting in the Lord. Isaiah 41:10 says, "Do not fear, for I am with you; do not be dismayed, for I am your God. I will strengthen you and help you; I will uphold you with my righteous right hand" (NIV).

We are also warned of the danger of living in fear, as it can lead us away from living in faith. Proverbs 29:25 shouts, "Fear of man will prove to be a snare, but whoever trusts in the Lord is kept safe" (NIV). We must learn to trust the Lord in all of life's circumstances so that we can live without fear and worry.

Pray:

El Deah, thank You for Your promise that we do not need to fear or be anxious. Help me to live in faith and trust You and Your plan for my life. In Jesus' name, amen.

Further reading: Isaiah 41:10, Proverbs 29:25, 2 Timothy 1:7, Romans 8:15, Psalm 56:3, Isaiah 26:3, Psalm 27:1, Deuteronomy 31:8.

Ponder:

- ☐ How can I face my fears in faith and not give in to worry and anxiousness?

- ☐ What fears am I currently facing?

- ☐ What is the difference between being aware of potential risk and living in fearful anticipation of the worst?

My reflection.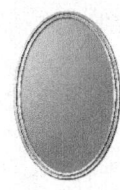

The thoughts that stood out to me are: DATE _____

Bible Devotional Guide Day 28:

Topic: **Redemption**

Read: **Ephesians 1:7 NIV**

Key Verse:

"In him we have redemption through his blood, the forgiveness of our trespasses, according to the riches of his grace."

Apply:

We live in a broken and hurting world and often struggle with the effects of sin, failure, and hopelessness. Fortunately, our God is a God of redemption. The Bible tells us that God sent His Son, our Lord, and Savior Jesus Christ, to redeem us from all our sins and restore us to a relationship with Him. This is the redemption of scripture, and it is a beautiful display of God's love and mercy towards us.

God's plan of redemption is one of the most beautiful mysteries of the Bible. Every single Christian can find beauty and comfort in their redemption story. In God's plan of redemption, we can learn that He has paid, freed, and restored us from the damages of sin and so each one of us can be made new again. God's redemption comes through failed relationships and sin. Sin can often lead to us feeling isolated, out of touch, and out of step with our relationship with God.

The good news is that no matter what we have done, we can be redeemed. God desires that we be reconciled to Him because that is the only way we can experience ultimate peace and joy. God accomplished redemption through Jesus' death on the cross. Jesus' death atoned for our sins, making it possible for us to draw near to God. In other words, Jesus paid the price for our sins so that we could be forgiven. The Bible says that Christ offered Himself as a sacrifice so that we could be cleansed from our sins and become a "new creation" (2 Corinthians 5:17, KJV).

The Bible tells us that redemption is an act of grace, and we owe our salvation to the blood of Christ. His sacrifice on the cross provided the atoning price for our sins, and we are now able to come to God in repentance and faith. By believing in the work of Christ on the cross, we are forgiven and made right with God. This is the purpose of redemption, and it is a beautiful display of grace and love from our heavenly Father.

Pray:

Immanuel, thank You for Your great love and mercy. Your plan of redemption is a testament to the depths of Your love for us. Thank You for sending Your Son to pay the price of our sins on the cross. Help us to remember the importance of Your sacrifice and to live out the reality of Your redemption. Enable us to spread the good news of salvation to others. In Jesus' name, amen.

Further reading: John 3:16-17, Romans 3:23-24, Colossians 1:14, 1 Peter 1:18-19, Revelation 5:9-10.

Ponder:

☐ Have you ever doubted your right standing with God?

☐ Do you believe that God forgives you of your sins?

☐ Are you still struggling with the effects of sin?

My reflection.

The thoughts that stood out to me are: DATE

La'Tosha M. Aikens

Bible Devotional Guide Day 29:

Topic: Purpose

Read: Jeremiah 29:11 NIV

Key Verse:

"For I know the plans I have for you," declares the Lord, "plans to prosper you and not to harm you, plans to give you hope and a future."

Apply:

The idea of purpose is something we all struggle with at some point in our lives. We want to feel like we have meaning in this world, an impact and that there is something special we are here to do. And the Bible has a lot to tell us about what this purpose is and why it matters. The Bible starts with the story of God creating the world and everything in it, and throughout the Bible, we see that God has uniquely created each of us with an individual purpose.

God's plans for us may not be the same as our plans, but He wants us to live out our lives with purpose and meaning. God desires to place a purpose in our lives and shape our character. He wants us to be intentional in how we live, to make an impact on the world around us. In the Bible, we learn what God's purpose for us is—to do His will and fulfill His plan for our lives. Romans 12:2 teaches that renewing your mind and aligning your life with God's will are crucial steps in fulfilling your purpose. The more you seek God's will and allow Him to transform you, the more clearly you will understand and step into the unique calling He has for you.

God calls us to be faithful and obedient to Him. He desires us to be a light in the darkness and shine the truth and love of Jesus to a world in need. God desires us to have a purpose so that we can live with passion and joy, free from fear and despair. But living this purpose in faith and obedience is easier said than done; it's going to take hard work. We must be intentional about our spiritual lives.

We must learn to pray and study the Bible, spend time with godly friends, and seek God in all our decisions. God has placed us here for a purpose, and the more we make a conscious effort to live this purpose out in faith and obedience, the more we will experience the joy of fulfilling God's plan for our lives. So let's commit to pursuing our purpose and fulfilling God's plan for us.

Pray:

Messiah, thank You for the gift of life and the purpose You have placed on it. Help us to live out our lives with meaning and purpose, knowing that it is much bigger than ourselves. Guide us and equip us in the way we should go, and may our lives be a testimony of how You have worked in us. In Jesus' name, amen.

Further reading: Isaiah 54:2, 2 Timothy 4:7-8, Ephesians 2:10, Philippians 1:6.

Ponder:

- ☐ Do you believe you have a purpose in life? Do you know what it is?

- ☐ What do you feel makes life worth living?

- ☐ Do you ever feel lost or that you don't know what to do with your life?

My reflection.

The thoughts that stood out to me are: DATE _____

Bible Devotional Guide Day 30:

Topic: **Grace**

Read: **Ephesians 2:8-9 NIV**

Key Verse:

"For it is by grace you have been saved, through faith—and this is not from yourselves, it is the gift of God— not by works, so that no one can boast."

Apply:

Grace is an act of unmerited kindness that is extended to us by God. As human beings, we can't earn grace and it isn't deserved; rather, it is freely given to us by our loving Creator. We see throughout Scripture how God pours out His loving kindness and mercy in the form of grace. It is grace that brought salvation to all people (Romans 6:23). It is grace that enables us to do all things through Christ, who strengthens us (Philippians 4:13).

Understanding the role of God's grace in our lives is vitally important to us as believers. As we grow in our wisdom and knowledge about the grace of God, we experience His grace at work in our lives in ever-increasing magnitude. Because of God's grace, we can do all things through Him, no matter how impossible a task may seem to us by our own strength. It is God's grace that enables us to live in righteousness, so that we may become more Christ-like and live a holy life.

God's grace also strengthens us to persevere in difficult times. His grace is an unfailing source of strength in our moments of weakness, giving us the ability to stand strong and fully endure adversity. His grace is a shield that protects us from whatever is not of God (2 Thessalonians 3:3) and gives us the grace to forgive and extend grace to others (Matthew 6:14).

By dwelling in God's grace, we can uproot any seeds of doubt and fear and bring forth a harvest of joy and love. We are so blessed to have such an amazing God who is so rich in grace and mercy. There is a reason the Bible tells us multiple times to be filled with His grace (Psalm 84:11, 2 Corinthians 13:14). We will never be able to exhaust His grace, and it will keep sustaining us for all eternity.

Pray:

El Chuwl, thank You for the amazing grace that You pour out on us. We are so blessed to have such a loving and compassionate God. Help us to always stay rooted in Your grace and to extend grace and mercy to others. In Jesus's name, we pray. Amen.

Further reading: Romans 5:17, Romans 12:6, 1 Peter 5.

Ponder:

☐   What is grace?

☐   How does grace benefit us as believers?

☐   What can we do to take full advantage of God's grace?

My reflection.

The thoughts that stood out to me are: DATE _____

_____

_____

_____

_____

_____

_____

_____

_____

_____

_____

_____

_____

_____

_____

_____

_____

La'Tosha M. Aikens

Bible Devotional Guide Day 31:

Topic: Selflessness

Read: Matthew 20:28 NIV

Key Verse:

"Just as the Son of Man did not come to be served, but to serve, and to give his life as a ransom for many."

Apply:

Being selfless in a world that frequently promotes selfishness can be difficult. However, as believers in Him, we have a responsibility to follow His example of selfless love and devotion. We must exhibit selflessness for several reasons. First and foremost, selflessness aligns with the very essence of our faith. Jesus, our ultimate example, displayed selflessness in its purest form. He willingly laid down His life for us, demonstrating sacrificial love and service. By imitating Christ's selflessness, we reflect His character and bring glory to God.

Selflessness can be powerfully shown through generosity. Bless others by sharing your time, talents, and resources without expecting anything in return, bless others by sharing your time, talents, and resources. Prioritize the needs of others. Put other people's needs before yourself. Make sacrifices and go above and beyond to assist someone who is in need. In your conversations, be nice and compassionate.

Here are a few doable strategies for developing selflessness: Embrace humility as you serve. In your daily activities, look for opportunities to help others. It could be serving your family with joy and humility, lending a hand to a neighbor, or volunteering in your community. Make a point of paying attention to what others are saying when you are conversing with them. Attempt to understand their needs and problems by demonstrating genuine concern and empathy.

Furthermore, selflessness fosters unity and harmony within the body of believers. When we prioritize the needs of others above our own, we create an environment of love, support, and mutual care. It strengthens our relationships and builds a sense of community, allowing us to fulfill the biblical command to "bear one another's burdens" (Galatians 6:2, KJV).

Pray:

Jehovah Shammah, thank You for the example of Jesus, who selflessly served and gave His life for us. Help me to grow in selflessness and to imitate His love in my daily life. Give me a heart that is sensitive to the needs of others and a willingness to serve them with joy and humility. Fill me with Your Spirit, Lord, so that I may reflect Your selfless nature in all that I do. In Jesus' name, amen.

Further reading: Philippians 2:3-4, Galatians 5:13, Romans 12:10, 1 John 3:16, Mark 10:45, Luke 6:38, 1 Peter 4:10

Ponder:

- ☐ What does this reveal to you about the importance of selflessness in the life of a follower of Christ?

- ☐ What does true selflessness look like in your life daily?

- ☐ How does God's love for you influence your ability to love others selflessly?

My reflection.

The thoughts that stood out to me are: DATE _____

_____

_____

_____

_____

_____

_____

_____

_____

_____

_____

_____

_____

_____

_____

_____

_____

Topic: **Sin**

Read: **Romans 6:23 NLT**

Key Verse:

"For the wages of sin is death, but the free gift of God is eternal life in Christ Jesus our Lord."

Apply:

Sin is a reality that plagues humanity. It separates us from God, damages our relationships, and brings forth various consequences. However, as believers, we don't have to remain trapped in the cycle of sin. Through Jesus Christ, we can find forgiveness, healing, and the strength to break free from its grasp.

To break free from the struggles of sin, we must start by acknowledging the reality of our sinfulness. It's important to honestly examine our hearts and actions, identifying areas where we have fallen short of God's standards. This self-reflection helps us to recognize our need for God's forgiveness and transformation.

Next, we must humbly confess our sins to God. Confession involves coming before God with a contrite heart, admitting our wrongs, and seeking His forgiveness. God's promise in 1 John 1:9 assures us that if we confess our sins, He is faithful and just to forgive us and cleanse us from all unrighteousness. Embracing this truth allows us to experience the freedom and restoration that comes through God's grace.

Breaking free from sin also requires an intentional pursuit of righteousness. We need to actively cultivate our relationship with God through prayer, studying His Word, and seeking His guidance. As we draw near to Him, He empowers us through His Holy Spirit to resist temptation and make choices that align with His will. This ongoing relationship with God strengthens us and provides the tools we need to overcome sin.

Finally, surrounding ourselves with a supportive Christian community is crucial in our journey toward freedom from sin. Connecting with fellow believers who can provide accountability, encouragement, and wise counsel helps us stay on the path of righteousness. Together, we can spur one another on to love and good deeds and bear one another's burdens.

Pray:

Jehovah Tsuri, we come before You acknowledging our sinfulness and our desperate need for Your forgiveness. Grant us the humility to recognize our faults and the strength to break free from the struggles of sin. Fill us with Your Holy Spirit, guiding us into a life of righteousness and holiness. Thank You for the gift of Your grace and redemption. In Jesus' name, we pray. Amen.

Further reading: Romans 3:23, Psalm 51:1-12, Galatians 5:16-25, Ephesians 4:22-24, 1 Peter 2:24, 1 John 1:8-10.

Ponder:

- ☐ What does sin mean to you and has it affected your life?

- ☐ How does God's forgiveness and grace offer hope amid our sinfulness?

- ☐ How does the reality of God's forgiveness and grace give you hope when you fall into sin?

My reflection.

The thoughts that stood out to me are: DATE _____

_____

_____

_____

_____

_____

_____

_____

_____

_____

_____

_____

_____

_____

_____

About the author

La'Tosha Aikens is a writer, speaker, and passionate believer who has experienced the transformative power of God's grace in the midst of life's emotional struggles. Through personal experiences, prayer, and biblical wisdom, she equips readers with practical tools for emotional healing and spiritual growth. La'Tosha deeply believes in the power of God's Word to heal, deliver, restore, and guide us on our journey.

As an inspired author, La'Tosha's heartfelt writing illuminates the life-changing impact of God's Word. With a deep love for the Lord, she invites readers on a spiritual journey that encourages faith, healing, and discovery.

Her influential voice resonates with profound meaning, inspiring hearts and encouraging a closer relationship with God. La'Tosha's books serve as guiding lights, offering wisdom, inspiration, and a deeper understanding of faith to all who read them.

Recognized for her contributions to spiritual literature, La'Tosha's words uplift, inspire, and transform lives. She leads her readers to embrace God's teachings and experience His grace, spreading love, faith, and understanding through every page. La'Tosha leaves an indelible mark on the hearts and souls of her readers, helping them walk in God's truth and love.

Closing thoughts

As you close the pages of this devotional, I pray that the words you've read have touched your heart and inspired you to draw closer to God. My hope is that through these reflections and truths, you've found a renewed sense of purpose, strength, and peace in your journey. Remember that God's love, grace, and wisdom are always available to guide you through every season of life.

May you continue to seek Him daily, trusting that He will lead you, heal you, and empower you to fulfill the beautiful purpose He has designed for your life. Keep His Word close to your heart and know that you are never alone on this journey. He is with you, every step of the way.

Thank you for allowing me to walk alongside you through this time of reflection. May God's peace, joy, and love overflow in your life, and may you experience His transforming grace in every area.

Blessings,

La'Tosha